Reflections for the Effective Nonprofit Chairperson

A volume of the Effective Philanthropy and
Fund Raising series.

Reflections for the Effective Nonprofit Chairperson

Quotes, axioms and observations to help you lead our important institutions

Jim Norvell

Writers Club Press
San Jose New York Lincoln Shanghai

Reflections for the Effective Nonprofit Chairperson
Quotes, axioms and observations to help you lead our important institutions

Writers Club Press
an imprint of iUniverse, Inc.

For information address:
iUniverse, Inc.
5220 S. 16th St., Suite 200
Lincoln, NE 68512
www.iuniverse.com

Artistic license was exercised with the quotes borrowed from an illustrious array of thoughtful people. Insertion of their observations in juxtaposition to my own was based on their unique similarity, often taken out of context. Those who are still around to do so are free to do the same with mine.

ISBN: 0-595-20878-9

Printed in the United States of America

A Pivotal Role

It matters little how successful you are in your daily pursuits; when a nonprofit organization asks you to chair its board, you had better feel a little inadequate. Beware if it is only honorary. An organization worth your good name had better be serious about what it does. You should be expected to lead, to make things happen and to maintain control – all with very constrained and widely shared authority. You must be judicious in your acceptance because an important institution will rise or fall on the quality of your commitment.

Nonprofits emerge and are sustained by people who care enough to volunteer non-refundable time, share their financial resources and lend their influence. In thousands of interviews with nonprofit participants, I have found that they rely on the character of the organizations' governance boards far more than on the skill of the staff. One of the first documents a prospective donor or leader asks to see is the roster of board members. They look for signs of strength and accomplishment. They will invest only where the prospects of success are high.

As a board chair, your most important role is to ensure that those expectations are met in deed and in spirit. You must shape the board so that its capabilities meet the organization's needs and so that individual board members have the opportunity to utilize their talents in meaningful roles.

Your first duties as chair are to assure governance that will provide strong, ethical policy and sound financial support for the executive and staff. You must have a strong ambition for the organization but allow the chief staff officer to create and pursue his or her own vision. If you have a high public profile and a commanding public presence, you can help with image building and articulation of the executive's vision; if you do not, you can enable others in these roles. The effective chair balances the skill and acumen of the staff with the power and authority of the board - a delicate equilibrium between empowering and leading.

The very best of you check your egos at the door. While it is important to command the respect of the chief executive officer, the chair must advise the executive as a colleague, not a minion. If you use the office to advance your own agenda, you will undermine the executive's authority and de-motivate staff.

Never shy away from the opportunity to use your abilities and influence on behalf of important nonprofits, but be sure that you are willing to give them the full measure of your attention. They deserve it.

Jim Norvell

For Jason and Adam
For my sons, Jason and Adam, both of whom have the compassion and can-do attitudes that will serve them well if they ever have the honor of chairing a nonprofit organization.

To serve is beautiful, but only if it is done with joy and a whole heart and a free mind.

Pearl S. Buck

Quotes, axioms and observations to help you sustain our important institutions

This book was compiled as a resource for nonprofit board chairs to learn some of the key lessons I have found to be useful in governing nonprofit organizations. It also provides some thought-provoking quotations that may be used in various pieces of organizational literature to motivate volunteers and staff. Finally, I wrote it because I like quotes and have found that many of you share that enjoyment.

Power is not inherently bad.

Power does not corrupt man; fools, however, if they get into a position of power, corrupt power.

George Bernard Shaw

Power has many faces and forms.

*With an eye made quiet
by the power of harmony,
and the deep power of joy,
we see into the life of things.*

William Wordsworth

Power has a negative connotation but
nothing good would ever happen without it.

I know of nothing sublime which is not some modification of power.

Edmund Burke

Personal power is not important unless you want to accomplish something.

Happiness is in action, and every power is intended for action; human happiness, therefore can only be complete as all the powers have their full and legitimate play.

David Thomas

Everyone has a power base built on ability, knowledge, relationships and authority.

If money is your hope for independence you will never have it. The only real security that a man can have in this world is a reserve of knowledge, experience and ability.

Henry Ford

How you look is not easily changed, but how you are seen easily can be.

Life consists not of holding good cards,
but in playing those you have well.

Josh Billings

Hard work gains respect; respect is power.

To be somebody, you must last.

Ruth Gordon

Many types of power are used to coerce, but others provide a gentler, surer influence.

Being powerful is like being a lady. If you have to tell people you are, you aren't.

Margaret Thatcher

Taking advice can boost power or diminish it depending on the source of the advice and its frequency.

Advice is what we ask for when we already know the answer but wish we didn't.

Erica Jong

Good fundraisers possess expert power.

But where's the man who counsel can bestow, still pleas'd to teach, and yet not proud to know?

Alexander Pope

Wealth often signals power, but not unfailingly.

Money hasn't really been an issue for me for quite a while. I just do what I feel like—that's all there is to do.

Jack Nicholson

Everyone possesses power to some degree and uses it both well and poorly.

There is no knowledge that is not power.

Ralph Waldo Emerson

Power must be used by a nonprofit for tactical advantage.

There is no meaning to life except the meaning that man gives his life by the unfolding of his powers.

Erich Fromm

An organization without power is doomed.

To be weak is miserable,
Doing or suffering.

John Milton

The practical expression of power is leadership, but the possession of power does not insure leadership.

Power?
The only power I've got is nuclear—
and I can't use that.

Lyndon Baines Johnson

The chief executive must be the initial change agent.

Imagination is the highest kite you can fly.

Lauren Bacall

Learning to be a good manager is much more difficult than learning effective fund-raising technique.

Some people are so busy learning the tricks of the trade that they never learn the trade.

Vernon Law

Style is an important element of leadership.

Every man of action has a strong dose of egoism, pride, hardness, and cunning. But all those things will be regarded as high qualities if he can make them the means to achieve great ends.

Charles DeGaulle

The skilled executive makes only those decisions that cannot be delegated.

No easy problems ever come to the President. If they are easy to solve, somebody else has solved them.

Dwight David Eisenhower

A leader is a symbol as well as a participant.

I was not the lion, but it fell to me to give the lion's roar.

Winston Churchill

Building shared vision is the leader's primary role.

The only limit to our realization of tomorrow will be our doubts of today.

Franklin D. Roosevelt

Complex decisions are seldom made without a high reliance on intuition.

The heart always sees before the eye can see.

Thomas Carlyle

Intuition is one of a leader's most important assets.

Seeing's believing, but feeling's the truth.

Thomas Fuller

Leaders inspire by communicating an exciting organizational future.

Our chief want in life is somebody who will make us do what we can.

Ralph Waldo Emerson

The best executives have a vision and a charisma that motivate peak performance.

If you have anything really valuable to contribute to the world it will come through in the expression of your personality.

Bruce Barton

The quality of staff is an accurate reflection of leadership.

To be an effective leader you have to turn all your so-called followers into leaders.

David C. McClelland

A strong leader's influence is sometimes gained more readily by keeping them out of the limelight.

I have had enough.

Golda Meir

The more powerful the leadership, the higher the motivation.

Winning isn't the only thing but wanting to win is.

Vince Lombardi

The board members' highest duty is to insure their organization operates above all applicable laws.

In the search for ways to maintain our values and pursue them in an orderly way, we must look beyond the resources of the law.

Dean Acheson

Someone has to show the way for others.

Do it big or stay in bed.

Opera promoter Larry Kelly

Leadership can make or break a campaign and its participants.

A team should be an extension of the coach's personality. My teams were arrogant and obnoxious.

Al McGuire

Strong boards are fund-raising boards.

A few highly endowed men will rescue the world for centuries to come.

John Henry Newman

A strong board is an accident without a good nominating committee.

Quality is never an accident; it is always the result of high intention, sincere effort, intelligent direction and skilled execution; it represents the wise choice of many alternatives.

Will A. Foster

If the board chair will not lead, who will follow?

I have always had a dread of becoming a passenger in life.

Princess Margrethe of Denmark

Volunteers run from conflict.

Tranquility will roof a house, but discord can wear away the foundation of a city.

Ernest Bramah

A weak board is more damaging than a weak executive.

In rivers and bad governments, the lightest things swim at the top.

Benjamin Franklin

Weak boards generally come from weak chairpersons.

*When people are free to do as they please,
they usually imitate each other.*

Eric Hoffer

Board members provide leadership best through planning, stewardship and evaluation.

As for him who voluntarily performs a good work, verily God is grateful and knowing.

The Koran, Ch. 2

No one solicits as effectively as a committed volunteer, only the chief staff officer is a close second.

Ya gotta do what ya gotta do.

Sylvester Stallone (as Rocky Balboa in "Rocky IV")

No paid employee carries the credibility
of a committed volunteer.

You give little when you give of your possessions. It is when you give of yourself that you truly gain.

Kahlil Gibran

The inequities of life demand
philanthropy.

We must build a new world, a far better world—one in which the eternal dignity of man is respected.

Harry S. Truman

Social consciousness is the first step in a philanthropic solution.

We must have the press of the crowd to draw virtue from us.

Angelo Patri

If the gift does not affect the donor's life, it is merely a handout—not philanthropy.

Do not be conformed to this world, but be transformed.

Romans 12:2 (NRSV)

Philanthropy is created by the same
drives that fuel competition.

All of our dreams can come true—if we have the courage to pursue them.

Walt Disney

Most philanthropy is based on emotion.

Emotion has taught mankind to reason.

Marquis de Vauvenargues

Philanthropy is the socialism of democracy.

Whoever has two coats must share with anyone who has none; and whoever has food must do likewise.

Luke 3:11 (NRSV)

The more social freedom we experience,
the greater our need for philanthropy.

I believe we are here on planet earth to live, grow up, and do what we can to make this world a better place for all people to enjoy freedom.

Rosa Parks

Philanthropy is second only to the vote in symbolizing democracy.

Money spent on ourselves may be a millstone around the neck; spent on others it may give us wings like eagles.

Roswell Dwight Hitchcock

Philanthropy alone cannot bridge all social inequities; but, with government as an ally and enabler, it can minimize them.

Giving away a fortune is taking Christianity too far.

Charlotte Bingham

The quality of life in the United States would be unexceptional without philanthropy.

If there is one word that describes our form of society in America, it may be the word—voluntary.

Lyndon Baines Johnson

Philanthropy is a quid pro quo transaction.

As the purse is emptied, the heart is filled.

Victor Hugo

Altruism is more likely to appear as instinctual heroism rather than charity.

There are two perfectly good men; one dead and the other yet unborn.

Chinese proverb

A philanthropic transaction is a valuation and an exchange.

Decide what you want, decide what you are willing to exchange for it. Establish your priorities and go to work.

H. L. Hunt

Self interest regulates all transactions, philanthropy included.

A man does not have to be an angel to be a saint.

Albert Schweitzer

The philanthropic exchange is not always apparent.

A bone to the dog is not charity. Charity is the bone shared with the dog, when you are just as hungry as the dog.

Jack London

Negotiation is common in major philanthropic transactions.

Let every eye negotiate for itself
And trust no agent.

William Shakespeare

The apparent motivation for generosity may be misleading.

Take egotism out and you would castrate the benefactors.

Ralph Waldo Emerson

Jim Norvell

Altruism is highly overrated.

Every major horror in history was committed in the name of an altruistic motive.

Ayn Rand

The Philanthropic Sector is a response
to life's inequities and the need to serve.

Life has no meaning except in terms of responsibility.

Reinhold Niebuhr

Social consciousness is at the root of philanthropy.

We will have to repent in this generation not merely for the vitriolic words and actions of bad people, but for the appalling silence of the good people.

Martin Luther King, Jr.

Philanthropic acts stem from resonance between the needs of others and personal value systems.

Many organizations are very clear about the needs they would like to serve, but they don't understand these needs from the perspective of the customers.

Philip Kotler

Philanthropy is a gift on one side and a promise on the other.

*A mind conscious of integrity scorns to say
more than it means to perform.*

Robert Burns

Everyone has needs that philanthropy meets.

Trouble is a part of your life, and if you don't share it, you don't give the person who loves you enough chance to love you enough.

Dinah Shore

Nonprofit privilege and huge revenue
streams make philanthropy an inviting
target for government control.

Those who worry about the motives of the charitable bolster their own political attitudes or comfort themselves with their own miserliness.

Benedict Nightingale

Philanthropy is too often marketed only through fund raising.

I get fifteen or twenty letters a day for everything from Yugoslavian dog illnesses to marathon diseases. It numbs you. So you write off a check for twenty dollars to a charity to absolve yourself of guilt.

Anjelica Huston

Philanthropy is both a behavior and an ideal.

Be not merely good; be good for something.

Henry David Thoreau

Donors have rights that organizations should look upon as obligations.

There's no such thing as a free lunch.

Milton Friedman

Situational ethics aren't ethical.

I think its better to come in second than to be impeached.

George McGovern

Character is the expression ethical standards.

*In matters of style, swim with the current;
in matters of principle, stand like a rock.*

Thomas Jefferson

Commitment to ethical standards defines organizations and people.

If ever I said,
in grief or pride,
I tired of honest things,
I lied.

Edna St.Vincent Millay

Influential leaders shape the
organizational culture.

The manager administers, the leader innovates. The manager maintains, the leader develops. The manager relies on systems, the leader relies on people. The manager does things right, the leader does the right things.

Forbes Magazine

Nonprofits must abide by ethical standards in a much more public way than private sector organizations.

Many people like to believe charities as dishonest as they are supposedly mismanaged. They actually prefer them that way, because it means that they do not have to feel guilty about their own lack of generosity.

Benedict Nightingale

Fund raising's fiduciary implications demand specific ethical standards of the highest magnitude.

The knights had to vow poverty, chastity, and obedience. They only kept the last vow.

Gen. George S. Patton, Jr.

Ethics are a contract between the
organization and its constituents.

I only know that what is moral is what you feel good after and what is immoral is what you feel bad after.

Ernest Hemingway

Ethical conduct is influenced, but not guaranteed by standards.

My best friend is the one who brings out the best in me.

Henry Ford

The highest ideals demand the highest
standards of conduct.

The ultimate test for us of what truth means is the conduct it dictates or inspires.

William James

About the Author

James R. (Jim) Norvell

Jim is a second-generation fundraiser who began his career immediately after graduating from Southern Illinois University—Edwardsville. He served in annual fund positions at Monticello College, the Foundation for Independent Colleges of Pennsylvania and Washington University before joining G. A. Brakeley & Co., Inc., Los Angeles, as a capital fundraiser. He left Brakeley to form his own capital campaign consulting firm, Development Management Associates, Inc. (DMA) and to earn his MBA at UCLA. Over fifteen years, he and partner Bob Zuer expanded DMA to $2 million in annual billings, serving clients throughout the Western United States, Great Britain and Australia.

0-595-20878-9